Hair on Fire

Hair on Fire

Afghan Women Poets

CALICO

Hair on Fire is twelfth in the Calico Series.

Two Lines Press
582 Market Street, Suite 700, San Francisco, CA 94104
www.twolinespress.com

ISBN: 978-1-949641-84-4

Cover design by Crisis
Cover image © Hangama Amiri
Typesetting and interior design by Marie-Noëlle Hébert

Printed in the United States of America

Library of Congress Cataloging-in-Publication Data available upon request.

THIS BOOK WAS PUBLISHED WITH SUPPORT
FROM THE NATIONAL ENDOWMENT FOR THE ARTS.

Aria Aber

Toward a Decentered Poetry

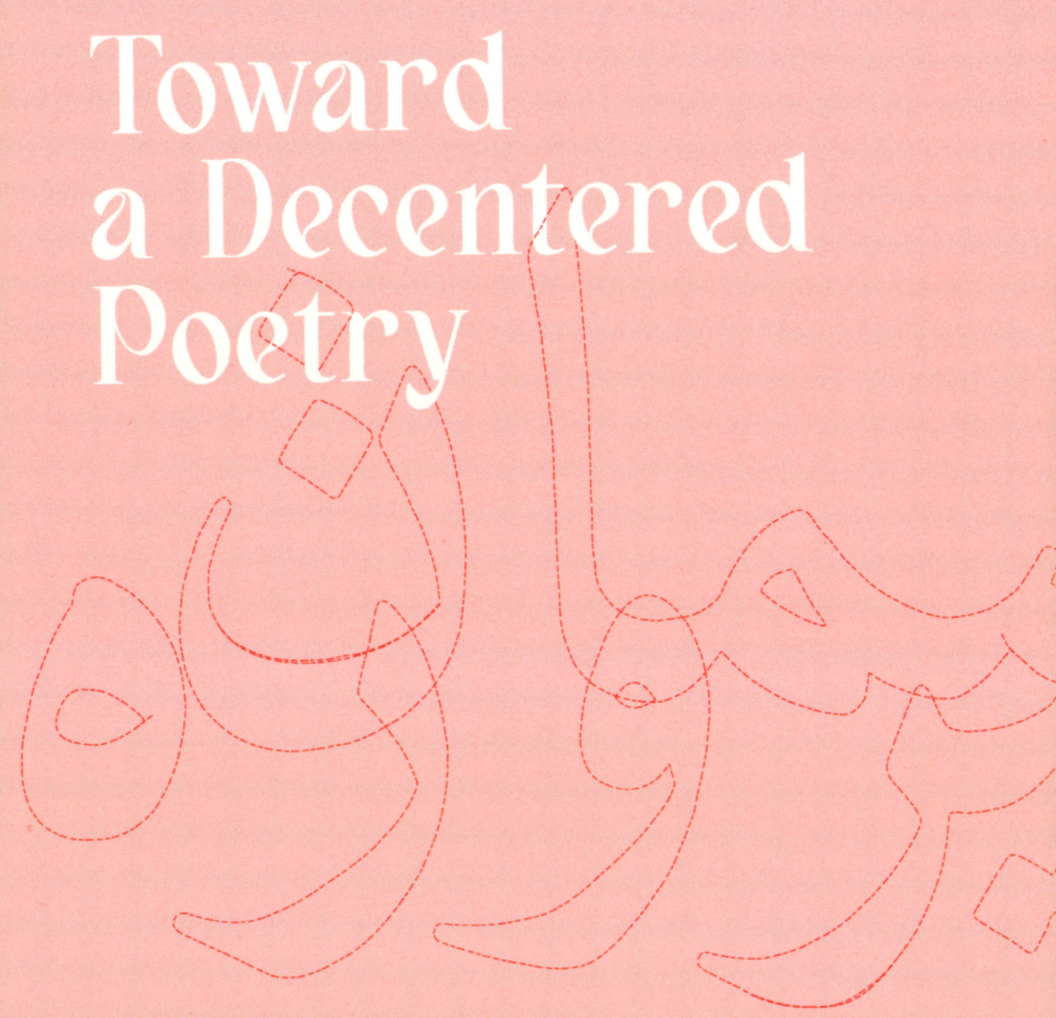

In late October 2023, during the early stages of the genocidal siege on Palestinians, I encountered a video on Instagram user John Rizkallah's page, which showed footage of his 2010 family vacation to Gaza. The intimate montage cuts from people of all ages in gardens, kitchens, and living rooms, talking and playing games, preparing picnics, laundry pinned to a clothesline, to shots of streets bustling with cars and trucks; natural landscapes and summer skies; and children jumping from walls. I watched this reel countless times on repeat, crying in front of the screen. Whenever I didn't scroll through social media, Telegram channels, or Al Jazeera for live updates of the exponentially rising death toll of civilians, many of whom are children, I returned to his page to rewatch the video. Egyptian–Libyan singer Hamid El Shaeri's song "Ayonha" plays in the background, accentuating the wistful sense of freedom and ease. There is nothing special about this one-minute-twenty-second-long video—it just depicts everyday scenery. And yet, the mundanity of this stranger's life is what moved me. The tenderness and ennui of a normal, anonymous, civil life—offset from the center of visual slaughter we saw in the media—broke open a part within me that had hardened and become hopeless and cynical, allowing me to access the depths of my grief.

I hadn't experienced this sense of grief since the fall of Kabul in 2021, nor had I felt the call to action, to organization, to collective activism. I returned to the video because it showed regularity among ruins, even in what we might call an open-air prison. The color palette—yellow, ochre, saturated blue, the grainy light—reminded me of the pictures I took during my trip to Kabul in 2019. I saw my family and my friends reflected in Rizkallah's video. I saw myself in the face of the bored girl who responds "It's fine" when the man behind the camera asks how her first day in Gaza has been going. This is me, I thought, meaning: This could've been me if I hadn't grown up as the child of Afghan refugees in Germany. I remember texting my Somali-American friend, the writer Asiya Gaildon, and asking her what our lives would have looked like if our families hadn't been expelled from their native lands and torn apart by war. What themes would our work have circled? What images, what textures, what music? We would have written different books, I am sure, not novels and poetry collections that interrogate warfare, foreign policy, and the horrors and pathos of displacement. Consider the lines ending one of Mahbouba Ibrahimi's poems, tr. Zuzanna Olszewska, which resonate so deeply with my own grief:

> Regret
> exile
> aloneness
> I did not deserve these.
> My poems should have borne
> the scent of redbud and oleaster
> the tinkle of anklets and attans
> the tang of sheep's milk in green thickets.

But as it is, I am, first and foremost, a writer of exile. I write in a country, in a language, that is not my own. I know I am not alone in this. As the poems in *Hair on Fire* evince, the fate of the exiled Afghan woman writer is commonplace, even if she continues to write in her native tongue. But it's also a fate that expands beyond Afghanistan, a fate that is shared among many countries and diasporas. In his essay "Reflections on Exile," Edward Said quotes Wallace Stevens to posit that an exilic life is governed by a "mind in winter." Temporality is ruptured, the exile's "life is led outside habitual order. It is nomadic, decentered, contrapuntal." And this is how I experienced my condition and that of those around me. It is from this point of rupture that I am writing, reading, and thinking about poetry. A point of decentralization, frayed at the fringes.

The concept of the contrapuntal, which Said refers to, comes from musicology, and describes two interdependent or independent musical lines coexisting in one piece. The plurality of two songs—the song of here, and the song of there—makes up the DNA of the exilic writer. To some extent, I also find it a helpful concept to frame a translated anthology such as *Hair on Fire*. The poems here exist side-by-side, in the original and in the English translation; somewhere between those two languages, a life of hope and possibility is transmuted. The poem emerges to voice two realities, which may be at odds with each other or harmonize, and may even touch. In Ibrahimi's poem "Footprint" (tr. Fatemeh Shams and Armen Davoudian), for example, "آسمان فیروزه" becomes "the turquoise sky." The Persian word for turquoise is "فیروزه" or "firuzeh," derived from the word "piruzeh," which means victory. Of course, this etymological root is lost in translation, but what the English word "turquoise" connotes is closer to the reality of displacement: it comes from the French word for "Turkish" and refers to the import of the gemstone from Ancient Persia through Anatolia to Europe. In this single adjective two realities, two histories, coalesce. The meaning itself becomes contrapuntal.

**

Despite being fluent in both English and Persian, I hesitate to claim to belong to a group or to speak with authority on the subject of "Afghan Women Poets." It would be more precise, perhaps, to locate the fraught first-person plural in the global diaspora: a "we" among those diasporic readers and writers among us who feel more comfortable reading the translated poems in this anthology, rather than the original. But I also know that a designation such as "Afghan women's poetry" necessitates the examination of canonization. After all, T.S. Eliot calls poetry "the soul of the nation." Thus, the question of Afghan poetry brings up the question of unity. What constitutes literary unity among a people who are as diasporic as Afghans? There are about nine million Afghans living in the diaspora; many more are the descendants of earlier refugees, just like myself. We have a country, yes, but our country has been under occupation since 1979. And like my family, I refuse to acknowledge both the past and current Taliban regimes as a "free government," instead considering them another occupational force. A regressive, tribalist, segregationist occupation. One that has been funded by states that don't have the Afghan people but their own agendas in mind, leading back to the destabilization of the Soviet Union in the 1980s, as supported by the covert CIA program Operation Cyclone under the reign of Jimmy Carter and Ronald Reagan.

Afghan poetry, therefore, is by default a poetry of fragmentation, multiethnic positionalities and languages, and geographic variation. It is, essentially, a decentered poetry that begins with the rich literary heritage of Khorasan, with writers such as Rumi, and leads to martyred writers such as Nadia Anjuman and beyond, to the contemporary Afghan–American poet Sahar Muradi.

But this anthology is more distinct and feminist in scope, collecting the poetry of Afghan women written in Persian. Afghanistan is currently the only country in the world where girls are not allowed to go to school beyond sixth grade. Withheld from education, they are shunned into the confines of domesticity, imprisoned into the shadows of houses, eradicated from public life. The oppression of women is not something new, it's been ongoing for decades. But so is the resistance of Afghan women. My mother and aunts were feminist activists who were imprisoned because they were members of RAWA, the Revolutionary Association of the Women of Afghanistan, led by the martyred revolutionary Meena Keshwar Kamal, a young woman who fought for gender equality and women's rights. She was assassinated in 1987, but RAWA has been active since then, building schools and supporting the education of children in Afghanistan, and their work has spread to refugee camps in Pakistan and even abroad, in America and Europe, where they help resettle refugees.

The phrase "Afghan women's poetry" makes me think of oral histories, of secrets whispered in kitchens, jokes told in bathrooms. I think of rituals in wedding chambers and wedding jewelry gifted as an insurance to find a way out one day, just as Ibrahimi writes (tr. Olszewska): "my homeland / is still my mother / who sold all her wedding gold / to buy me a plane ticket / so I could go / and stay alive." I think of the Landay, the oral Pashto folk poem, which Eliza Grisworld and the Poetry Foundation honored in their 2015 issue of *Poetry Magazine*. I think of Nadia Anjuman, whose work is collected in this anthology, a woman who was killed by her husband. I think, of course, of Forough Farrokhzad, the Iranian poet who died young and who serves as an idol for many Afghan woman writers. I think of Nawal El Saadawi, the Egyptian feminist who Meena Keshwar Kamal modeled her life after. I think of radios and butterflies and children and walnut trees. I think of Meena secretly traveling to Valence, France, to represent the Afghan resistance movement at the French Socialist Party Congress in 1981 and taking on the Indian surname by which she is now known, so as not to be detected as Afghan. I think, in essence, of a solidarity that is global and international, that extends beyond national borders, artificial boundaries that are contested to this day.

This unifying marker of decentralization, of fragmentation, means that there is no typical Afghan woman writer just as there is no Palestinian or Egyptian or French one. Canonical categorization, especially by nationality, is an arbitrary measure that forecloses the possibilities of myriad creativity and diversity. One can study trends, tendencies, and aesthetic preferences. But even looking at the poems in this anthology, I am astounded by the vast array of thematic and aesthetic preoccupations, by voices that are aggrieved and exuberant, at times elegant and at others irreverent and erotic. Look at these lines by Maral Taheri (tr. Hajar Hussaini), for example, whose work is rageful, charged and surreal, riotous:

> this is not an aching
> *my father died and I am a whore*
> I have wrapped Van Gogh's severed ear in a handkerchief
> and I scream battle cries

Perhaps it's too simple of an argument to claim that the

poetry of Afghan women amid times of erasure and the illegality of women's education is an act of resistance. That writing in your native tongue is an act of cultural resurrection, a refusal of imperial warfare. But it's true that the claim to language at a time where women are silenced can be read as a scream for freedom, a claim to life. To write in the face of war, in the face of violence, in the language of your country, is a repudiation to eradication. As Karima Shabrang writes, in Sabrina Nouri-Moosa and Samantha Cosentino's translation:

> No one can stop tomorrow from coming,
> "and I don't care if they say
> my songs are useless."

Being part of a people who live with ruined archives, whose historical documents are classified or destroyed, whose houses and hospitals are bombed, whose universities are burned down, whose villages are erased off the map, means that no poem is "useless." I believe that even a poem can be read as a document, a point of witnessing human life on earth. "I never want to write another word about the war," Svetlana Alexievich wrote in her astounding book *Zinky Boys* (tr. Andrew Bromfield) about the fate of Soviet soldiers in Afghanistan during the 1980s. But what about those on the other side of the battlefield?

And those who were confined in the houses? What about the Afghan girls and women? Are they bored of war, of writing about it?

Poetry, to me, exists at an axis opposed to the imperial and colonial violence of nation states. In her essay "A Poetry of Proximity," the Iranian–American poet Solmaz Sharif says that poets are "the caretakers of language." That they must diagnose, detangle, and desist what despots and politicians ruin, in order to keep language from "calcifying." Like a poem that demystifies the calcification of language, that Instagram video was the antidote, the balm, to the visual syntax of how Arab and Muslim countries are portrayed in the West. Even when I turn to poetry for its potential to demystify the collusion of aesthetics and politics, I also dream of a world where poems can be about something else, about the mundane scenes in Rizkallah's home video; about the tenderness of the most innocuous human interactions; about a world where language is unscathed by genocide, warfare, and displacement. And the poets in *Hair on Fire* write in the same vein, with the same hope. Shabrang envisions a quiet life, contrapuntal to the violence of a ruined country:

> I return
> to the wildness of youth

to cafes at the end of the day
the back-to-back cigarettes of lonely afternoons
and cups
declaring my solitude—bitter, blatantly.

Language is the material with which we represent, question, and archive the world. We diagnose. But we also envision with language; we dream. I draw a point of solidarity between these contrapuntal points: Somalia and Palestine and Egypt and France and the United States and Afghanistan. I draw a connection between the streets of Tehran, where Ibrahimi's speaker wakes up, and the clavicle of the lover in Taheri's poem.

**

What drew me to Rizkallah's Instagram video, most of all, were the children. Their boredom, their innocence, their futures. I was reminded not just of myself, but also the young girls I met at an orphanage in Kabul during my first and perhaps only trip to Afghanistan in 2019. Our visit to the orphanage was at the tail end of the trip, but it was the most memorable experience of my two weeks. The orphanage was run by a socialist group and fostered a broad, artistic education for the young girls. A picture of Nadia Anjuman hung in the hallway, as did poems by Pablo Neruda, a quote by Maxim Gorky, and a painting of Che Guevara. The girls didn't wear headscarves, and didn't have a religious education. They learned English, they played instruments, they danced the attan, and they painted and sang. I left that visit with a secure hope in the revolutionary potential of art, language, and international solidarity. After the fall of Kabul, the orphanage was dissolved, as their socialist ideology made them a target under the Taliban. During August of 2021, I worked with several Afghan friends in the diaspora, all creatives and artists, to help get people out of Afghanistan. My job was to secure the evacuation of those girls. We stayed awake at night, speaking on the phone, filling out documents, trying our best to set up secret missions with US and European soldiers to get them across the border. Those girls dreamt of becoming artists and musicians and lawyers and poets. I don't know where most of them are right now—in Iran, in Tajikistan, in Albania, in Turkey, in the United States. I don't know if they write. I hope they do.

Mahbouba Ibrahimi

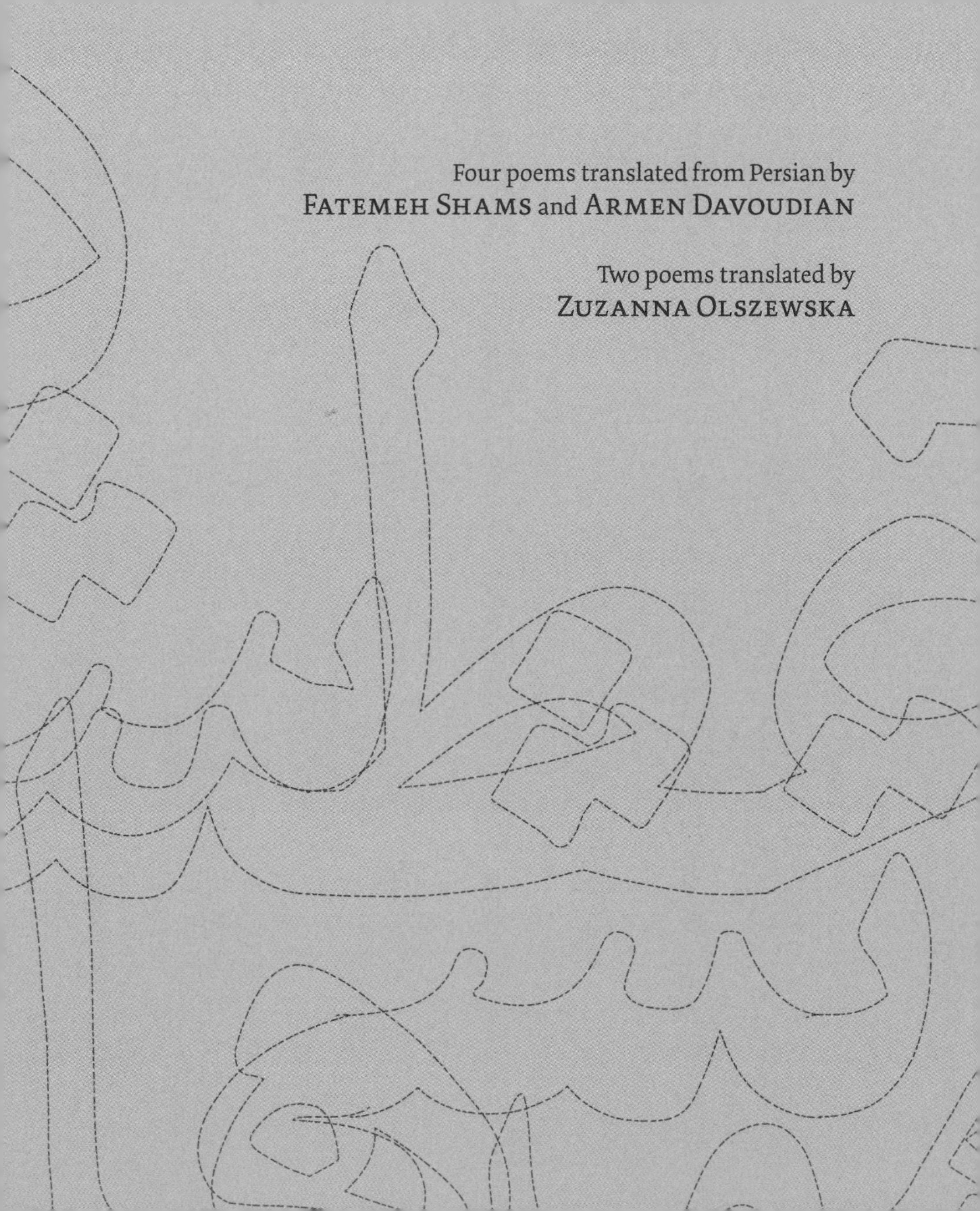

Four poems translated from Persian by
FATEMEH SHAMS and ARMEN DAVOUDIAN

Two poems translated by
ZUZANNA OLSZEWSKA

رد پا

در استکهلم
بیدار که می‌شدم
تنها بودم
در آغوش صبح
سپید
سرد
آفتاب
بر ته‌ریش طلایی‌اش
می‌درخشید
پلک که می زد
بر دریاچه‌ها موج می‌افتاد
بر دل من
اندوهی ناشناس

در پاریس
بیدار که می‌شدم
بی‌تقلّا

Footprint

Waking up in Stockholm
I was alone
in the arms of morning
blank
cold
the sun's blond stubble
glittered
every blink
sent waves over the lakes
an unfamiliar sorrow
over my heart

Waking up in Paris
I was a woman
without much effort
my hair fell in elegant curls
colors clung to my shirts

زن بودم
موهایم پیچ و تاب می‌گرفتند
رنگ ها به پیرهن‌هایم می‌چسبیدند
و شکوه گمشده‌ای
در ساق‌هام می‌دوید

در تهران
بیدار که می‌شدم
نبودم
یا بودم
تنها برای
رفیق خاکستری‌پوش خودم
که افسردگی‌اش را
چون‌رازی با من
در میان بگذارد

در کابل
خودم بودم
همین خودم
عصرها همیشه دلم می‌گرفت
به تلفن ها جواب نمی دادم
چراغ های خانه را خاموش می‌کردم
و در تاریکی

lost glory
ran through my ankles

Waking up in Tehran
I did not exist
or I did
only for my gray-clad comrade
so she could share
her depression with me
like a secret

In Kabul
I was myself
my own self
evenings my heart was heavy
I ignored the phone
I turned off the lights
and in darkness
listened to the sound of rockets
that burned my childhood

In my dreams
the corpses of the young kept walking
leaving their bloody footprints

به صدای راکت‌هایی گوش می‌دادم
که کودکی‌ام را در داده بودند

در خواب‌هام
جسد های جوان راه می‌رفتند
و رد پاهای خونی‌شان را بر ملحفه‌ها
جا می گذاشتند

در کابل
بیدار که می‌شدم
ملحفه‌ها را
می شستم
و خورشید
را به آسمان فیروزه ای‌ام
برمی‌گرداندم.

on my bedsheets

Waking up in Kabul
I washed the bedsheets
and returned the sun
to my turquoise sky

Translated by Fatemeh Shams and Armen Davoudian

کلمات سه‌گوش

یوز پلنگی که در تختخواب من بیدار می‌شود
می‌داند
امروز باید سریع‌تر از قطار بدود

به دخترم می‌گویم
برای جنگل
پوتین‌هایش را بپوشد
سربازها
باید بیش‌تر از خودشان مواظبت کنند

شیر می‌ریزم در گیلاس پسرم
از امروز روزها تاریک‌تر می‌شوند
ساعت‌های آفتابی
باید بیرون بازی کند

دهانم را در آینه نگاه می‌کنم
کلمات سه‌گوش

Jagged Words

The cheetah who wakes up in my bed
knows today it must run faster than the train

I tell my daughter to wear her boots into the forest
soldiers must take better care of themselves

I pour milk into my son's glass
the days will grow darker from today
he should play outside
while the sun shines

I inspect my mouth in the mirror
jagged words
fly out broken
slashing the edges of my lips

But one day

شکسته بیرون می‌پرند
و گوشه‌های لبم را زخم کرده‌اند

یک روز
اما
همه چیز بهتر می‌شود
و نوه‌هایم به یاد نمی‌آورند
پس از جنگی سخت
به دنیا آمده‌اند.

it will all get better
and my grandchildren will not remember
they were born
after a devastating war

Translated by Fatemeh Shams and Armen Davoudian

پازل

آدم‌های تنها
تنها که هستند
چه کار می‌کنند؟

من
می‌نشینم و پازل خودم را دوباره می‌سازم
اول‌از همه
آدمی را که قبلا ساخته‌ام می‌شکنم
بعد تکه‌هایش را به هم می‌ریزم
طوری که نتوانم راحت پیدایشان کنم

تکه‌های به هم ریخته‌ام
ناگهان
هوس چای می‌کنند

Puzzle

What do lonely people do
when they are alone?

I sit down and solve the puzzle
of myself again
first I break down the person I had solved previously
then I scramble the pieces
so that I can't find them easily

My scattered pieces
suddenly they are craving tea
step by step
all in a scramble
they rise up

سلانه سلانه
پخش وپلا
بلند می‌شوند
و از آشپزخانه
یک گیلاس چای می‌آوردند

انگشت‌ها
دنبال بندهای گم شده‌شان می‌گردند
کامل که شدند
صدای موزیک را بلندتر می‌کنند

لب‌هایم یکدیگر را جستجو می‌کنند
در تمام رنگ‌های سرخ
برای بوسه
نه
برای نوشیدن چای

با باقی مانده تکه‌ها
مصروف می‌شوم

سیاهی موهایم را
با سیاهی کفش‌هایم
اشتباه می‌گیرم
و بلند می‌خندم

and get a cup of tea from the kitchen

Fingers
search for their missing joints
and once complete
they turn up the music

My lips rummage through all shades of red
for each other
for a kiss
no
to drink tea

I busy myself with the remaining pieces
I mistake the black of my hair
for the black of my shoes
and I laugh out loud
my white teeth appear

I try not to remember my old form
my new form
the further from reality
the more entertaining

دندان های سفیدم پیدا می‌شوند

سعی می‌کنم به یاد نیاورم
شکل قبلی‌ام‌را
شکل جدید
هر چه از واقعیت دورتر
سرگرم کننده‌تر.

Lonely people
do all sorts of things
with their loneliness

Translated by Fatemeh Shams and Armen Davoudian

پروانه‌ها

موهای دخترم را شانه می‌زدم
در آینه
که ناگهان
دست‌هایم را دیدم
پروانه‌های سپید
کی از پیله‌در آمده بودند؟

انسان نخستین
آتش را
به تصادف
کشف کرد
من
زنانگی‌ام را
که
خون به شقیقه‌هام دوید
و
ناگهان

Butterflies

I was brushing my daughter's hair
in the mirror
and suddenly caught a glimpse of my hands.
When did white butterflies
emerge from their cocoon?

The first human being
discovered fire by accident.
I discovered my womanhood
after blood rushed to my temples
and suddenly grapes fell from the vine
and decided to turn into wine.

I was looking for a pen
to write this poem.

Colors and patterns returned to the walls of caves.

انگورها
از تاک‌ها ریختند
و به فکر افتادند
شراب شوند

دنبال قلم می‌گشتم
که این شعر را بنویسم

نقش‌ها و رنگ‌ها
بر دیواره‌ی غارها برگشتند

برای پیاده روی
به جنگل رفتم

درخت‌هارا دیدم
که تصمیم گرفتند
تخته پاره شوند
کشتی بسازند
به دریاها سرازیر شوند
و جزیره‌های ناشناخته را
کشف کنند

موهای دخترم را
در آینه

I went for a stroll in the forest.

I saw the trees
that decided to become planks
and build a ship
to sail the seas
and discover unknown islands.

I was brushing my daughter's hair in the mirror.
The butterflies were circling
and weaving the story of women's civilization.

Translated by Fatemeh Shams and Armen Davoudian

شانه می زدم
پروانه ها چرخ می‌زدند
و تاریخ تمدّن زنان را
سر رشته می‌کردند.

بازگشت

فکر می کردم
دهان خوشبوی عشق
بازوان محکم دین
و آغوش گرم وطن
نجاتم می دهد

حالا
سپاسگزار عشقم
که شکار بهتری یافت
دندان هایش را از گلویم
برداشت
و اجازه داد
عطر کاج ها را نفس بکشم

هر چه جان کندم
جایی در بازوان دین نیافتم
حرمسرا بزرگ بود
من

Return

I used to think
love's fragrant lips
the firm arms of faith
and the homeland's warm embrace
would save me.

Now
I am grateful to love
for finding better prey
taking its teeth off my throat
and allowing me
to breathe in the scent of the pines.

However hard I tried
I couldn't find a place in the arms of faith
The harem was big
I was wild
and I couldn't wait my turn

وحشی بودم
و نمی توانستم
برای معاشقه
به نوبت بایستم
از سنگسار
ترسیدم
قفل ها را
شکستم و
گریختم

وطن اما
هنوز
مادرم است
طلاهای عروسی اش را فروخت
برایم بلیط هواپیما خرید
تا بروم
زنده بمانم

یک روز
بی عشق
بی دین
فقط
به خاطر مادرم
بر می گردم

for lovemaking.
I was afraid of being stoned.
I broke the locks
and fled.

But my homeland
is still my mother
who sold all her wedding gold
to buy me a plane ticket
so I could go
and stay alive.

One day
without love
without faith
just
for my mother's sake
I will return.

Translated by Zuzanna Olszewska

زن - وطن

بمب ها و تفنگ‌هایتان را
زباله هایتان را
جمع کنید
و به خانه هایتان برگردید
مردم آسوده ی جهان !

چشم از آب و خاک ما بردارید
همسایه های نامهربان !

اندوهگین و خشم آلود
این روز ها
شعر
نمی تواند شاعرانه گی کند

اصلا کدام زن
دست و دلش
به موهایش می رود

Woman, Homeland

Take your bombs, your guns
and your trash
clear out and go home,
comfortable people of the world!
Stop eyeing up our water and land,
heartless neighbors!
Mournful, enraged,
these days
poetry
can't work its poetry.
Which woman
has the heart
to tend to her looks
when she's anxious and distraught?

A woman
abandoned by all

وقتی آشفته و نگران است ؟

زنی
که همه گان
ترکش کرده اند
زن نیست
باروت فشرده در گلوی تفنگ است
غم سنگ شده
در سینه کوه

چگونه شعر بگویم
با این همه سنگ مذاب
در گلویم ؟

ما سزاوار جنگ نبودیم
وطن جان !
زن زیبای وحشی !

سهم تو
کاروان هایی با بار ابریشم و نور بود
انعکاس صدای رباب در کوهستان
برف سالنگ
آب گوارای هلمند
و مردان نیرومند مهربان

is not a woman.
She is gunpowder stuffed down the throat of a gun,
a sorrow petrified
in the mountain's heart.
How can I speak poetry
with all this molten rock
in my throat?

We did not deserve war,
homeland dear.
Wild, beautiful woman!
Your fate could have been
caravans bearing silk and light
The rubab's echoes in the mountains
Salang's snow
The Helmand's flow
and strong, kind men
who gifted you children
whose eyes shone with love and wisdom.

Regret
exile
aloneness
I did not deserve these.

که به تو فرزندانی
هدیه می دادند
که نور عشق و دانایی در چشم هاشان
می درخشید

من سزاوار حسرت نبودم
سزاوار آوارگی
تنهایی

باید شعر هایم
عطر ارغوان و سنجد می داشت
صدای پای‌زیب و اتن
طعم شیر گوسفندان بیشه های سبز

سبز می شود
یک روز
این همه آرزو
که در سینه خاک دفن کرده ایم

My poems should have borne
the scent of redbud and oleaster
the tinkle of anklets and attans
the tang of sheep's milk in green thickets.

They will grow green, one day,
all these dreams
that we have buried in the breast of the earth.

Translated by Zuzanna Olszewska

Maral Taheri

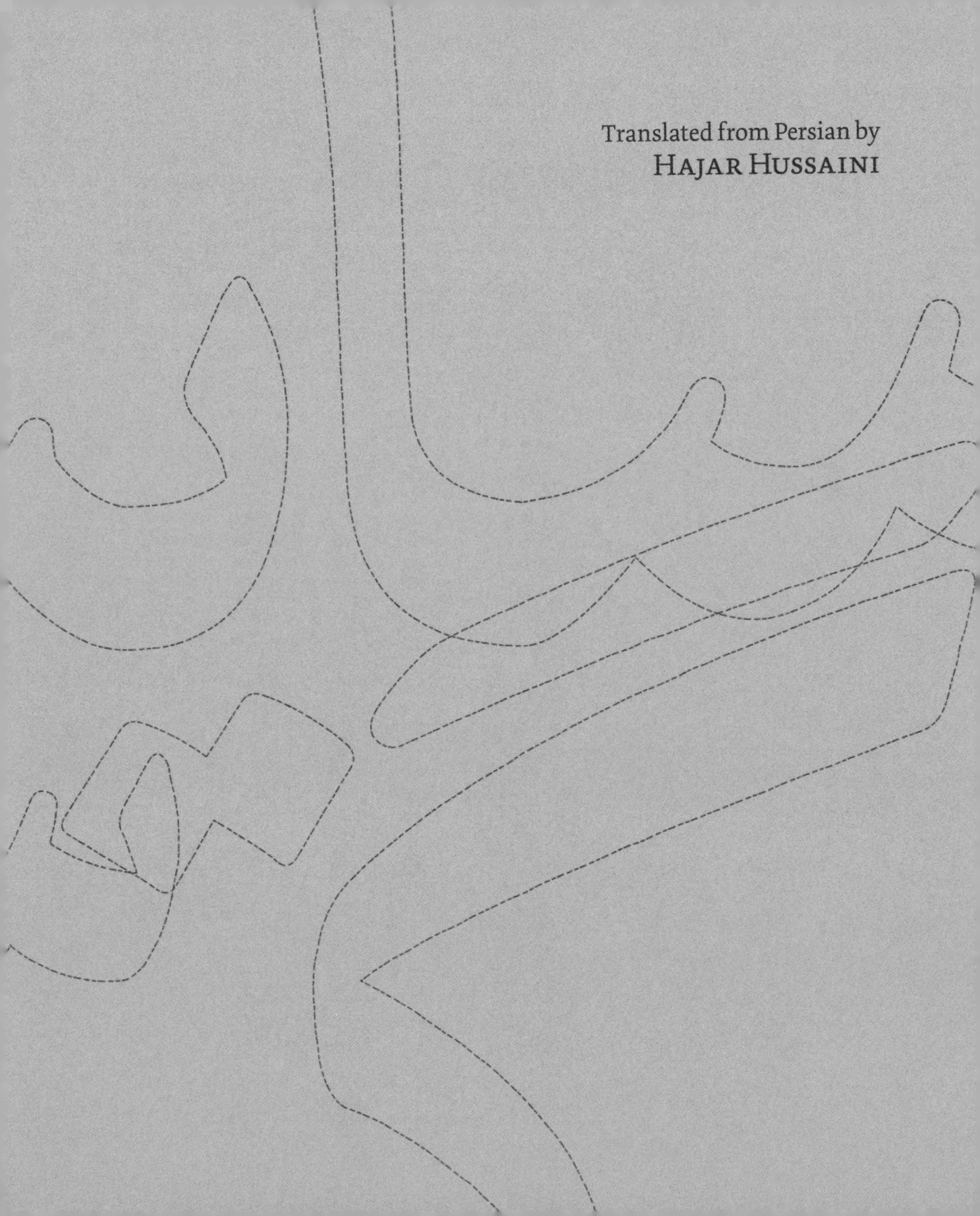
Translated from Persian by
Hajar Hussaini

سکس سایبری در مواجه با مرگ پدر

این یک پیپ نیست!
دنده‌ی چپ مردی‌ست که به دندان گرفته له له می‌زنم تا ته مزار
کنار تلِ خاکی که می‌پاشیدند رویِ بزاق یک میت
اِسمَع، اِفهَم، یا فلان بن فلان!
گوشت را در هذیان می‌خوابانند یک شب
از این پهلو به آن پهلو تلقین می‌دهند روی قلاده ای غمگین
گوشت برشته می‌شود
از بوسه می‌افتد به جان دادن
مقابل مرد سکسی سایبری که ناخنت را از ریشه درآورده

نزدیک‌تر نیا
سرت را پایین بگیر و به لوله فالوپ خیره شو
من از انجماد جنین‌های اجاره‌ای می‌ترسم
از باز و بسته شدن مدام آفتابگردان لابلای شکاف‌های شبانه!
فوبیای شبیه سازی فالوسی‌ام باش
که از یاس و لمس متورم خواهد شد
هرگز تا به امروز دردی شبیه من دیده ای؟

Cybersex in the Face of My Father's Death

this is not a pipe
it's a man's grumpiness, his left rib
that I carry between my teeth till I arrive gasping at his gravesite
next to the dirt mound they spread saliva over the corpse
listen, understand, the offspring of so and so
they lay the flesh down in delirium one night
from left to right they persuade us over his sad collar
the flesh roasts
from a kiss, one begins to die
across from the sexy man online
who pulls out a nail from its bed

don't come any closer
and keep your head down to gaze at the fallopian tube
I'm afraid of frozen embryos-for-sale
afraid of the constant opening and closing
of the sunflower at nightfall

باید یخ زده باشم که بوی تناسخ را در حرارت آفتابگردان حس نکرده ای

این یک درد نیست!
پدر مرده است و من یک هرزه‌ام
گوش بریده‌ی ونگوگ را لای دستمال پیچیده‌ام و جیغ‌های معرکه‌ای می‌کشم
انگار با همه‌ی بی‌شرف‌های شهر خوابیده باشم
و تنهایی‌ام را روی تخته گوشت تشریح کرده‌ام
از اشتهای خون خودم می‌ترسم
هندزفری را که فرو میکنم در گوشم جریان خون شدیدتر می‌پاشد در لحنم
چرا بند نمی‌آید؟
به هر طرف که نگاه می‌کنم ردِ کلمه‌هایم پاک نمی‌شود؟

نخواه از من که بغلت کنم
حس لامسه کار زیادی از پیش نمی‌برد
وقتی نمی‌توانی پیپ‌ام را پر کنی
پوستم را چگونه بلیسم و به پاهات فکر نکنم؟
به ران‌هایم
که وقت مردن پدر غمگین بودند و مضطرب
مثل خارپشتی زبر که دست هیچکس به داغی‌شان نمی‌رسید
و تو دیوانگی عریانی که در اندوهم بود را نترسیدی
تمام ترس‌هام را تنهام
چطور می‌شود از جنازه‌های جنین خوار نترسید؟
از مرگ نترسید؟
از عشق نترسید؟

so be my phallus phobia
which swells when touched and in despair
have you ever seen an aching akin to mine?
I must have turned to snow if you can't sense the scent
of reincarnation in the sunflower's heat

this is not an aching
my father died and I am a whore
I have wrapped Van Gogh's severed ear in a handkerchief
and I scream battle cries
as though I have slept with every reprehensible person in this city
I scribble down my loneliness on a cutting board
I fear my own bloodlust
when I put in earphones, I hear the curdling blood in my tone
but why won't it stop flowing?
no matter where I look
the traces of my words are not being erased

don't ask me to hold you in my arms
touch won't take us that far
when you can't fill up my pipe
how can I lick my own skin and not think about your feet
and my legs
they were anxious and sad in the face of my father's death

مرا به رشته‌های صدایت ببند و با فیبرهای نوری شلاقم بزن
رام کردن زنِ سرکشی در من به استعاره‌ی اُدیپی پدر وابسته نیست!
خیسی آفتابگردان ربطی به گوش بریده‌ی ونگوگ ندارد
نویزِ نام خانوادگی در نطفه‌هایی که به جای تو گاز می‌گیرند
سفارَش کرده ام گوشت‌های این جنازه را با مال تو لابلای هم چرخ کنند
تا خیانت کنم به مخاطب

این یک شعر نیست!
کلمات هم علیرغم میلم عاشقانه نشد
یک نفر این پیپ را از من بگیرد و پر کند...

like a prickly hedgehog who no one touched to sense its fever
and you weren't afraid of the naked madness in my sorrows
I'm alone with all my fears
how could someone not fear the corpse-eating fetus?
how could someone not fear dying
and loving?
tie me to your vocal cords and whip me with optical fibers
taming the defiant woman in me has nothing to do with an oedipal metaphor
the wet sunflowers have nothing to do with Van Gogh's severed ear
the noise of the surname is in the embryo that bites me instead of you
in my will, I've asked them to grind the meat of this corpse with yours
so that I can cheat on my reader

this is not a poem!

words, against my will, never line up so beautifully
someone should take this pipe from me
someone should fill this thing up

و شعر میتوانست زخمی باشد که هیچگاه سر باز نکند

باید یکی از ما دو تن صندلی را می‌کشیدیم
با تیغ‌های پنهان در مشت
چکاوک‌های غمگین زیر پیراهن
تو طناب می‌بافتی
و همسایه‌گان
رَج‌های لباس‌های زمستانی را با دندان‌های سرخشان می شکافتند
یکی از زیر، دو تا از رو
دو تا از زیر، سه تا از رو
و ماهواره هر هشت دقیقه کاندوم‌های تاخیری را تبلیغ می‌کرد
از حمام بوی گوشت پخته می‌آمد
درخت ها اعدام ها را اعلام می‌کردند
و کِرم ها از گنبدهای کبود به کوچه دویدند
باید یکی از ما دو تن عجله می‌کرد
ما عجله‌ای نداشتیم
مرهم روی زخم می‌گذاشتیم و همدیگر را می‌لیسیدیم
ملافه را می‌کشیدی روی پاهام
روی زانوهام

The poem could have been a wound that never opens to ooze

one of us should have pulled the chair
with sad larks buried in their shirt
hiding a knife in their fist
instead you wove a rope
and neighbors unraveled the yarns of
winter garments with their crimson teeth
one from below, two from above
two from below, three from above
the satellite tv was advertising discounted condoms in eight-minute intervals
the smell of boiled meat came from the bathroom
and the trees announced the execution schedule
worms rushed out of turquoise domes and into the streets
one of us should have hurried then
but we didn't
instead we dressed our wounds and licked each other off
you pulled the sheet over my bare feet
over my knees

روی خونابه‌ی وخیمی که از دوش نشت می‌کرد
توده ها احمقند می دانی!
با مرده باد زودتر به ارگاسم می‌رسند
و چشم بندهای مشکی
سورپرایزهای بزرگی دارند
گره‌اش که باز شود
معشوقه‌ات را می‌بینی نشسته وسط دادگاه
سربازها را سر به هوا می‌کند و سر به سر ساطورها می‌گذارد
سر بچرخانی صندلی را می‌کشد از زیر پاهات
می‌لولد بین لولوها...
نگران نباش عشق من
عشق خنگ من
من خیانت به خود را خوب بلدم
یک میراث فرهنگی‌ست که از کشورم به من رسیده
زیرخاکی و اصیل
شبیه همین خدا
خائن خوش لباس
که شریک دزد بود و رفیق قافله
و البته ما تعظیم نمی‌کردیم
لزومی نیست همیشه طبیعی و وفادار بود
خوشبخت و خانگی و خدا دوست
خو گرفته به خروارها درد که از آسمان به ما رسیده
چه اتفاق دیگری ممکن بود بیفتد؟
خدا چه خیالی برای خوشبختی‌ام داشت که خودکشی‌ام

and over the blood draining from the shower
the masses are idiots, don't you see?
they get off faster with *death to*
and black blindfolds make for bigger surprises
because when the knot's untied
you see your lover sitting in the middle of a court
flirting with soldiers and shooting the shit with an ax
the second you turn your head they pull the chair out from under you
and then your body worms its way toward the boogeymen
love, don't you worry
my stupid love
I know how to betray myself
it's a cultural heritage from my country
a buried treasure
humble and original, just like this god,
a traitor in fine clothes
both confidant to the thieves and companion
to the caravan
of course we didn't bow down
there was no need to look natural or act loyal
no need to be happy, homely, and god-loving
used to the substantial pain descending from the sky
what else could possibly happen?
what happiness could god imagine for me that suicide can't?

نداشت
من زخم خودم بودم
با شیارهای عمیقی که روی عشق سر باز می‌کرد
کافی بود یکی بگوید دوستت دارم!
تا خونم بپاشد بر پیراهنش
کافی بود یکی بگوید درخت
تا بگویم چیزی که می‌خواهم یک طناب حسابی‌ست
حساب کلماتی که به تنم میمالی به کنار
حساب بلندگوها به کنار
حساب لولوها با لوله‌های نشانه به سمت مغز هم به کنار
تکه پاره‌های مرا جمع نکن و بگذار حواسم به همه چیز باشد
گوش کن!
اعتقاد به کشتن هر هشت دقیقه کاندید می شود
باید یکی از ما دو تن صندلی را می‌کشیدیم.

I am my own wound
a deep cut that opens for love
it's enough for someone to say *I love you*
for my blood to gush onto their shirt
it's enough for someone to say *trees*
for me to say all I want is a reliable rope
then I'll forget about the words you rub on my body
I'll forget about the loudspeakers for a while
and I'll forget about the boogeymen and the barrels pointed at the brain
you don't need to pick up my pieces
let me tend to everything
listen...
our trust in killing is running as a candidate in eight-minute intervals
one of us should have pulled the chair

بغلم کن

بغلم کن
تنها چسبیده به تو از چیزی نمی‌ترسم
فکر می‌کنم به تمام چیزهای قشنگ
به عروسکم
که سوال‌های سخت نمی‌پرسد
به پسرم
که مرا به مادرش ترجیح داده
به خانه‌های خالی جدول
کتاب‌های ذبح نشده
نشئه‌های مخدر
مردهایی که دوستم دارند و تو کورشان کرده‌ای
مردهایی که دوستشان دارم و تو کورم کرده‌ای
می‌خواهم توی بغلت به دیگران فکر کنم
ببوسمت
و ماشه را بچکانم توی حلقات
تا لعنتی بمیری
احمق!

Embrace me

only glued to you am I not afraid of anything
only glued to you
do I think about nice things
like my doll
who never asks difficult questions
like my son
who prefers me to his mother
like the empty squares in a crossword puzzle
the unslaughtered books
the high of addict men who love me and are blinded by you
men whom I have loved and you have blinded me
I want to embrace you and think of others
I want to kiss you
and pull the trigger in your throat
die
you idiot!
Idiocy is enough for men

احمق بودن برای مردها کافیست
تا من به کارهایم برسم
باید بلند شوم
نوار بهداشتی‌ام را عوض کنم
عرق سوز زیر بغلم را دئودورانت بزنم
بروم بیرون در بایستم
به سمتی تف کنم
به سمتی ماچ
برگردم جدول‌هایم را پر کنم
هیچ وقت اعتراف نمیکنم جهان بی اهمیت است
من دقیقا همان چیزی را می‌بینم که زیر پوستم گلبول می‌شود،
مرد می‌شود، می‌زند از دهانم بیرون
باکتری می‌شود،
مرد می‌شود،
می‌زند از جایم بیرون
که بیرون منم
با چند میلیارد کوچولوی قرمز
که وسط ران‌هایم را چسبناک کرده اند
«مامان...مامان...ما رو نکش»
یا گوشه‌ی همین مبل قهوه‌ای دیوث
زانوهایم را بغل کنم
و انگشت‌هایم را یکی یکی آتش بزنم
به کرگدن دیوار روبرو خیره شوم
که با سرنگ

I need to get to work
I need to get up
I need to change my pad
I need to smear deodorant over my armpits' burning sweat
I need to go outside and lean against the front door
I need to spit to one side
and send kisses to the other
then come back and fill out my crosswords
I would never admit that the world has no meaning
I see precisely the things that are under my skin
that become a globule, become a man, burst from my eye
become bacteria, become a man, burst from my mouth
become a son, become a man, burst from my bed
for I'm standing outside
with a million of these small red things
between my legs, all sticky
"mom...mom...don't kill us"
next to this damn brown sofa
I should embrace my knees
set my fingers on fire
one by one
and stare at the rhino on the wall in front of me
with a syringe
I should spray a few ccs of obscenity into the air

چند سی سی فحش بپاشی به هوا
یا در حال التماس فرو بریزی
فرو رفتن را من تعیین نمی‌کنم
اما انتخاب نوع بستنی یا وقت حمام با من است
بستنی در حمام حال می‌دهد
زندگی بادکنک در سوراخ‌هایش
مرگ نامرد روی صندلیش
نامرد یعنی زن!
زنت می‌شوم
از این‌ها که توی یک اتاق، توی یک پنجره، توی یک ...
که روبرویت نشسته‌ام و لب نزده‌ام به چیزی
و دائم مواظبم که عاشقت نشوم
که دستم داغ نشود توی دستت
که ماشه را فرو کنم توی بینی‌ات
جمجمه‌ات از دهانت بریزد توی بستنی
یادم باشد از پسرم عذر خواهی کنم
که به بیهودگی دعوتش کرده‌ام
و از تو که به زن‌های دیگر فکر نمی‌کنی
اما من برای زن‌ها، نه بلیط می خرم
نه کف می‌زنم
نه نوشابه باز می‌کنم
و ترجیح می‌دهم مُرده‌ی مَردم را ببوسم
و از پنجره
به زن ها که لبه تخت‌ها نشسته اند

so…you can collapse in an act of supplication
I don't determine whether you fall
but the choice of ice cream or when to shower is mine
because having ice cream in the shower is great
the life of a bubble is realized through a poke
and the death of a coward ascertained on a chair…
being a coward means being a woman
…I'll become your woman
one of those still in a room—with a window—in a room
I'll sit in front of you without touching anything with my lips
I'm always careful not to fall in love with you
so my hands don't burn in yours
so I don't push the gun into your nose
so your skull doesn't spill from your mouth onto the cone
I must remember to apologize to my son
for I've brought him here in vain
I must apologize to you
because you never thought of other women
but I never buy tickets for women
I don't clap for them
or open their sodas
I prefer kissing my man's corpse and looking through the window
at other women who sit on the bed's edge
who jerk their legs

و پاهایشان را تکان می‌دهند
دست تکان بدهم
و این چاقو را فرو کنم توی چشم‌هایشان
که وقت بوسیدن چُرت نزنند
احمق بودن برای زن ها کافیست
بغلم کن
تنها چسبیده به تو از چیزی نمی‌ترسم
من ترس‌های کوچکی دارم
مثلا همین جن‌ها
با چادرهای مشکی
که از سر و کول هم بالا می‌روند تا صورتم را ببینند
لبه تخت ها نشسته اند و پاهایشان را تکان می‌دهند
مثلا همین خون‌ها که بستنی‌ام را شور کرده است
پسرمان
که بادکنک‌های سوراخ را دوست دارد
جدول‌هایی که من را در خودشان حل کرده اند
کرگدن دیوار روبرو
کتابهایی که ذبحم می‌کنند
جسدی که درحمام سوت می‌زند
بستنی می‌خورد
کور می‌کند
بغلم کن!

I wave at them
I want to push this knife into their eyes
so they stop nodding off mid-kiss
because idiocy is enough for women
embrace me
because only glued to you am I not afraid of anything
I have small fears
like these jinn
in their black chadors
who climb atop each other to get a glimpse of my face
who sit on the bed's edge and jerk their legs
like this blood that has spilled over my ice cream
and has made it sour
like our son
who loves perforated balloons
like the crossword puzzles that have solved me inside them
like the rhino on the wall
like the books that slaughter me
like the body in the bathroom that whistles and licks an ice cream
these things can blind a person
embrace me

Endnotes

In the poem "Cybersex in the Face of My Father's Death," the line "this is not a pipe" comes from the title of a painting by René Magritte and a book by Michel Foucault, both of which dwell on the treachery of images. "A man's grumpiness, his left rib" are both one phrase in Persian, "دنده چپ," with a double meaning; it refers to the biblical story of the creation of Eve out of Adam's rib, and is a colloquial saying for feeling a general sense of irritability. The line "listen, understand, the offspring of so and so" is my English rendition of the beginning line from the prayer "Du'a Talqin for the Deceased," traditionally recited at the burial site, particularly in Shi'a Islam to guide and affirm the deceased's faith after death. The line "my father died and I'm a whore" is from the film *Ma mère* (2004) directed by Christophe Honoré.

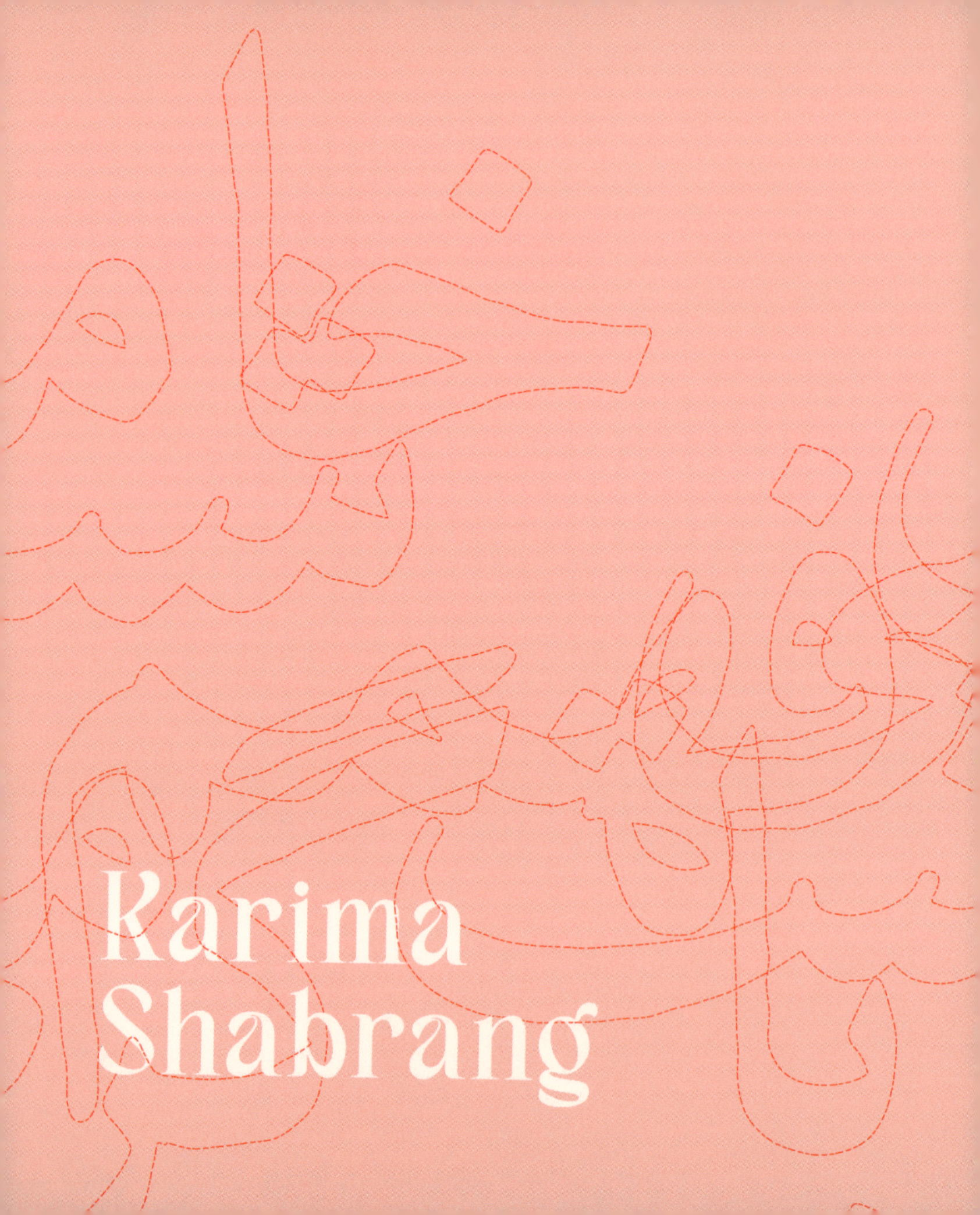
Karima
Shabrang

Translated from Persian by
SABRINA NOURI and
SAMANTHA COSENTINO

از هر چی خاموشی ست، می ترسم
از خاموشی شبانه کوچه ها
وقتی می فهمم
فردا وحشت می زاید
و آدم ها با گردن های دو کله
و دست های درازی که
تا ته زندگی همه
تا ویرانی باور من می رسد
از خاموشی کودکی در گهواره می ترسم
وقتی هر صبح چشم می گشاید
تفنگی روی دیوار صبح بخیرش می گوید جای پدر
و چند سالی بعد
جمع و ضرب را از زبان مرمی یاد می گیرد
و تفریق را از جای خالی همصنفانش
که دیشب جسد شدند
از خیره شدن به ریش بلند مرد ها میترسم
وقتی میفهمم

Of all things silent I am afraid,
of silent streets at night
when I know
that tomorrow will birth terror
and two-headed creatures
with long hands that reach
the bottom of every life
the end of my hopes.
Of the silent newborn I am afraid,
when he opens his eyes each morning
to find a rifle on the wall greeting him, not a father,
and a few years later
bullets will teach him to add and multiply
and missing classmates to subtract
those turned to corpses last night.
Of long hypnotic beards I am afraid,
when I know

فلسفه هر تارش دارهای دسته جمعی ست
از هر چی خاموشی ست می ترسم
از خاموشی خدا هم
که دست هیچ کودک یتیمی به گریبانش نمی رسد

in the thick plot of hair lies a mass execution.
Of all things silent I am afraid,
of a silent God
who dwells where the hands of orphans can't reach.

و عادت باید کرد
به بالا رفتن از پله‌های گناه‌آلود زمان
درد من همه از دست بلند و بی‌مایه‌ی روزگار است
چگونه می‌توانم زنده باشم
وقتی آزادی پروانه‌ی را که با عطرگیاه آمیزش عجیبی دارد
در چارراهی بزرگی به دار می‌آویزند
و گلوی مرا که
از پشت هفت کوه سیاه فریاد می‌زند
هنوز دستانی اند که محکمش می‌گیرند.
و عادت باید کرد
به مسافرت تلخ دستان خودم
که تنها خواب نوازش شانه‌هایت را می‌بیند
حضور تو که دل شب را
در اتاقم به تماشا فرا می‌خواند
چه بوسه و آغوش مقدس و پاکی
آیا خوش‌بختی در راه است که
دریغ و حسرت شب‌های بی‌تو ام را جبران کند؟

And I endure
climbing the sin-stained steps of time
with all my pain from fate's crass upper hand.
How can I live on
when the butterfly's freedom—her captivating, botanical scent—
hangs on the gallows at broad crossroads
and when my screams,
seven dark mountains away,
still die in my throat under their hands?
And I endure
the sad journey of my own hands
caressing your shoulders only in dreams
where the heart of night witnessed your presence—
what pure kisses, what sacred embraces!
Is happiness on its way
to reward me for my regretful nights without you?
We should tell them all

باید همه بدانند
که نطفه‌های من و تو
از بطن عشقی به دنیا آمده است
و بگو ما عشق را دوست می‌داریم
به اندازه‌ی یک هم‌آغوشی پاک
و چشم بستن جاویدانه
هیچ‌دستی راه فردا را مسدود نخواهد کرد
«و من نمی‌هراسم از آن که بگویند
ترانه‌های تو بیهوده است»

the seeds of life
are born in love's womb,
tell them we believe in love
even if only a pure embrace,
even with eyes closed for eternity.
No one can stop tomorrow from coming,
"and I don't care if they say
my songs are useless."

پیشترها
می‌خواستم در سی سالگی خلاصه شوم
غروب کنم در یک صبح مه‌آلود
عبور کنم زندگی را در اشک‌های مادرم
اندوه جاودانه‌ی شوم در نگاه پدرم
جسم سنگین باشم روی دوش برادرانم
آخرین بار نگاه کنم
با چشم‌های بسته به مهمان‌های اندوه‌گین
و مرگ تنها یارم شود

اما
امروز
امسال
جعرافیای ساخته‌ام به وسعت عشق
سرزمینی که
سال نو را با بوسه و آغوش شروع کنم
دوست دارم

Before
I wanted to be done with it by 30
to set during the early fog-filled hours
to dwell in my mother's tears
become an indelible sorrow in my father's eye
dead weight on my brothers' shoulders
and look around, with eyes closed, for the last time
at the mourning ones
and see only death beside me.

But
these days
this year
I have carved a geography as wide as love
a land
where I start the new year with kisses and embraces.
I return

برگردم به جنون جوانی
به قهوه خانه‌های آخر روز
به سیگارهای پیهم ظهر تنهایی
و پیاله‌های که
سکوت را تلخ و بلند فریاد می‌زد
تو را می‌خواهم
دوباره
در وقفه‌های اداری
در ساعات مزدحم روز
در کوچه های باریک
و ترس‌های نوجوانی
با من
شناور باش
مثل جویبارهای جاری
روی پل‌چک‌ها می‌نویسم
از دوست داشتن های دیوانه‌وار
می‌خواهم تاریخ شود
قدم‌های من
سایه‌های ما!

to the wildness of youth
to cafes at the end of the day
the back-to-back cigarettes of lonely afternoons
and cups
declaring my solitude—bitter, blatantly.
I long for you again
during work breaks
in the busy daytime hours
in narrow streets
and youthful worries.
Flow with me
in the rush of this river.
I'm writing on every single bridge
about love's madness.
I want my steps
and the shadow of us
to make history.

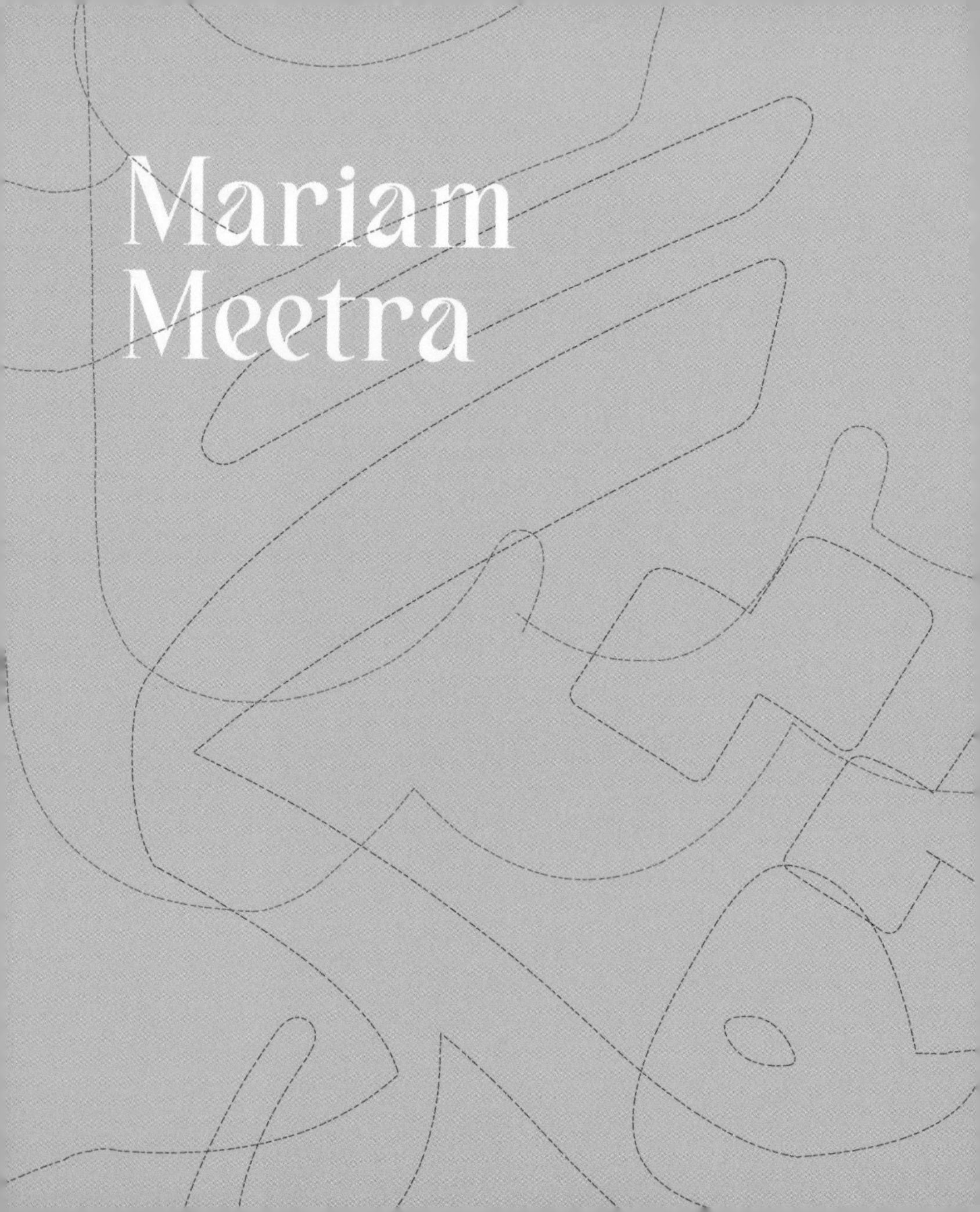

Mariam Meetra

Translated from Persian by
SABRINA NOURI and
SAMANTHA COSENTINO

بازگشت

جای خالی رودخانه ای هر روز ترک می خورد
در قلب من
با هر لبخندِ به تعویق افتاده
با هر شعرِ ناتمام‌مانده
با هر کلمه که می‌گریزد از سرم

در من رودخانه‌ای خشکید که
صبح ها با صدایش بیدار می‌شدم
عصرها در کنارش شعر می‌خواندم
حالا شب‌ها
دست می کشم
بر ترک های زمینی خشک
در تاریکی

قول می‌دهم
اگر برگردم
این بار پنجره را باز بگذارم

Return

The empty bed that was a river
suffers new cracks each day
in my heart
with every deferred smile
with every unfinished poem
with every word escaping my mind

A river has run dry in me
mornings, I'd wake to its song
afternoons, I'd write poems at its side
now, each night,
my hand traces
the cracks of this dry land
in the dark

I promise
if I ever return

درختی بکارم وسط اتاق
که انفجارهای خیابان نلرزاندش
بوی خون
دماغش را خشک نکند
و ریشه‌هایش آتش نگیرد
پرده ها را کنار بزنم
بگذارم باران نیمه شب به خانه بیاید
و آفتاب صبح دوباره بتابد
بر باغچه‌ی مهربان کودکی
برگردم و کمی بخوابم
بی اضطراب گم شدن
بر شانه‌ی روهایای شفاف دخترکی
در دوردست

I'll leave the window open
and plant a tree in the middle of the room
so the explosions can't shake it
the blood stench can't smother it
and the flames can't set its roots on fire
I'll draw the curtains
so night rain can come in
and the morning sun can shine again
in the tender garden of childhood
return to rest for a while
without fear of being lost
on the banks of a little girl's see-through dream
some place far away

شکستگی عمیق

چه فرق می کند
چند سال گذشته؟
هنوز کنار رویاهایم می خوابم
که دست برنمی‌دارند از سرم
و شب ها به خانه‌ای فکر می‌کنم
که چراغ‌هایش خاموش می‌شود
به سیاهی مطلق پشتِ پنجره فکر می‌کنم
نگران دخترانی
که چشم‌های روشن شان هر شب
از خانه دورتر می شود

صدای شکستن شیشه‌های خانه‌ای در دوردست
خوابم را می‌شکند
و ردِ عمیقِ شکستگی
پیوسته بر چهره‌ی روزهایم پیداست
هزارسال هم که بگذرد
به یاد خواهم آورد

Deep Break

What difference does it make
how many years have gone by?
I still sleep next to those visions
that keep a hand on my head
and at night I think of a house
whose lights go out
I think of the complete darkness beyond the window
I worry about the girls
with their eyes aglow, each night
moving farther away from home

In the distance, sounds of shattering panes
break my sleep
and tracks from the deep break
rise to the surface of my days
even if a thousand years go by
I will remember

صبح پراضطراب یک روز زمستان را
و قلب لرزان زنی را که صبح
جای دیگر جهان می تپید
و شب با چشمانی پر از رویا و شک
جای دیگر جهان خوابش نمی برد

that frightful winter morning
in the early hours, the trembling heartbeat of a woman
somewhere else in the world,
who at night with eyes full of visions and doubts
somewhere else in the world now can't find sleep

سایه

هر صبح
زندگی پخش می‌شود بر کف اتاق
چون سایه‌ی ناشناس زنی نگران
راه گم‌کرده در بن‌بست
من هر صبح می‌ایستم
شانه به شانه‌ی اندوهی که
می‌تواند از دیوار بگذرد
کلید بچرخاند در سرم
و نبض زمان را در هم بریزد

در بن بست نیمه روز
در تلاقی تردید و بیگانگی
رو به روی خویش می‌ایستم
و زندگی را جمع می‌کنم از ازدحام اتاق
به خیابان می برم
میان آدم‌ها
و هر روز تکه‌ای از آن گم می‌شود

Shadow

Every morning
life spills across the floor of the room
like the shadow of a nameless woman in agony
lost at a dead end
I find myself standing each new day
shoulder to shoulder with a sadness that
permeates the walls
turns a key in my head
and plays havoc with the beat of time

At a midday deadlock
at the confluence of doubt and distance
face-to-face with myself
I gather up life from the brimming room
take it onto the streets
into the crowds
where every day
a small piece of it leaves me

عطشزار

آتشی در موهای تو شعله‌ورست
که می ترساند سرزمین مردان را
و دچار سوختن می‌کند گندمزاران تشنه را
در عطشزار بی‌باران
تنها موهای تو آتش نگرفت!
مردان خشمگین بر تاکستان‌های شمال هم
آتش افروخته‌اند
انگورهای نورس تاکستان های سرزمین مادری
هنوز در آتش‌اند
و بوی موی سوخته‌ی دختران کوهستان
از سینه‌ی تاریخ بلندست هنوز
حرف که می‌زنی در آن آتش‌زار
همیشه از سوختن می ترسد صدات

Barren Plain

Your blazing mane
bewilders the land of men
and condemns the parched wheatfields to burn
in the rainless barren plain
it is not only your hair on fire!
in Shamali, hateful men have set the vines on fire
the young grapes of my motherland on fire
the scorched smell of country girls' hair
rises from the breast of history even now
in this fire-field, should you say something
you fear burning your tongue

Nadia Anjuman

Translated from Persian by
DIANA ARTERIAN
and MARINA OMAR

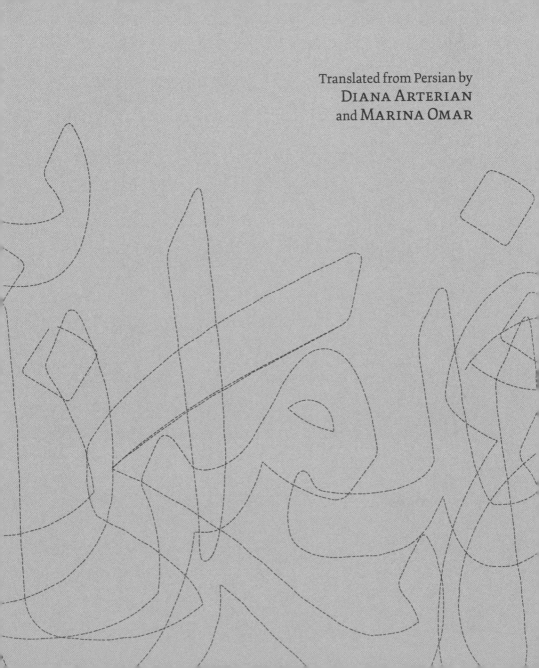

بازیچه

ای جعبه خالی از عروسك
ای هسته خود زدست داده
ای پا و سرت دریده، خسته
درکنج زباله دان فتاده

دیروز ترا به ناز بسیار
بنشسته به تخت طاق دیدم
اندام ترا درست و کامل
زیبنده یك اطاق دیدم

آن پیکر کاغذین و رنگین
همشانه جامهای زر بود
چشمان نیازمند طفلان
بر قامت تو نظاره گر بود

یکباره تنت به دست تقدیر
از اوج روانه شد به پستی

Plaything

Oh, empty doll box
Oh, you've lost your core
Oh, your doll's top and bottom are torn and ratty
tossed to the edge of the trash heap

Yesterday you were up on the shelf
I saw you, smug
your form whole
I saw you brighten the room

That papery, colorful box
next to gold cups
The groping eyes of children
gazed at you, top to bottom

Then your body was in fate's hands
You dropped from that height

من شاهد ماجرات بودم
دیدم که به سادگی شکستی

جسمی که درون پیکرت بود
با هرکه رسید دلبری کرد
بیخود شده با تماس هر دست
خندیده و خوش سخنوری کرد

با عشوه و ناز سرخوشانه
هوش از سرکودکان بدر برد
هم هستی خویش را تبه کرد
هم روح ترا به نیستی برد

آن جسم لطیف و نرم و زیبا
ازحجره خویش تا برون شد
یکدم به میان خاك غلتید
یك لحظه به چاه سرنگون شد

نه دست و نه پای دارد اکنون
نه تاج و نه موی چنگ در چنگ
برقامت او اثر نمانده
زآن جامه لاله ای خوشرنگ

در کشمکش میان طفلان

I saw your story
I saw how easily you broke

The figure inside you
charmed and flirted with anyone who passed
She laughed and chatted
intoxicated by the touch of hands

Flirty and pleased
her body stole sense from children
She ruined her life
and destroyed your spirit

That beautiful, soft, smooth body
as she emerged from her box
was suddenly rolling in the dirt—
then down a well in a second

Now she has no hands or feet
no crown or locks of hair
There is not a shred
of her bright tulip-red clothes

In the children's tussle

سر از تن او جدا فتاده
لیکن به لبش هنوز باقیست
آن خنده دلنشین ساده

جز پوچی و پایمال گشتن
فرجام چه شد تو را و او را؟
آخر به زباله ها سپردند
تندیس قشنگ آرزو را

اینک تو و پیکر شکسته
اینک تو و دستهای خالی
بازیگر هرزه زمانه
کی میشنود اگر بنالی؟

ای جعبه خالی از عروسک
من نیز تهی تر از تو هستم
بازیچه شدم به دست تقدیر
ناچیز شدم، به هم شکستم

دل از بر من جدا فتاده
افسرده و چاک خورده، خونین
پامال جفای دهر گشته
آن گنج گهرنشان رنگین

her head broke off—
but her lips still hold
that charming, simple smile

Aside from being emptied and trampled
what became of you two?
In the end they threw her away—
that beautiful statue of desire

Now you are this broken form
Now you are these empty hands
You are merely time's harlot puppet
Who will care to hear you whimper?

Oh, empty doll box
I too am empty—even more than yourself
I became a plaything in the hands of fate
I became nothing, I broke

My heart has fallen from me
withered, torn, and bloody—
my colorful treasure
trampled by the cruelty of time

بازیچه شدن حدیث تلخی است
جز محنت و درد سر ندارد
دستی که من و تو را تبه کرد
از ناله ما حذر ندارد

ای جعبه خالی از عروسك
ای هستهٔ خود ز دست داده
ای پا و سرت دریده، خسته
در کنج زباله دان فتاده

ثور ۱۳۸۱

To become a plaything is a bitter tale
It only brings trouble and misery
The hand that destroyed us
doesn't hear our whimpers

Oh, empty doll box
Oh, you've lost your core
Oh, your doll's top and bottom are torn and ratty
tossed to the edge of the trash heap

Sawr 1381 / Taurus 2002

طعم غزل

یک سبد دلهره ی شیرین
آه! فقط
یک سبد دلهره ی شیرین
کافیست که در فرداها
هستی کوچک من دیگر بار
در فضای غزلستان تبسم ها
آغاز شود
تا دلم باز شود

وای از حجم هجوم تلخی
باز هم زیر درختان حوادث خفتم
در کنارم سبدی لبریز است
و هنوز
هر که از طعم غزلهای من آگاه شود
چهره در هم آرد

۱۳۸۱

A Taste of Ghazal

One basket, sweet worry
Ah! Just
one basket, sweet worry
One is enough, so that tomorrow
my small life is once again
in the land of ghazals
                    where smiles emerge
                        and my heart opens

Ugh, such an attack of misery
I slept under the tree of disaster again
So beside me a basket overflows with doubt
And yet
anyone who knows the taste of my ghazals
                    will furrow their brow

1381 / 2001–2002

ایکاش

الا ای دختران انزوای قرن
ای راهبان ساکت بیگانه با مردم
ای مرده در آیین لبهاتان تبسم
بیصدا در کنج مهجوری خزیده
با تبار خاطرات خفته در انبوه حسرتها
اگر در لابلای یادها لبخند را دیدید
بگوییدش:
تمنای شکفتن نیست لبها را
ولی ای کاش در جریان اشک آرای نجواهای مان
گاهی
سخن را جلوه کمرنگ میبخشید

قوس ۱۳۸۰

If

Oh daughters of a century's seclusion—
Oh mute nuns, strangers to humanity,
Oh with smiles dead to the religion of your lips—
you silently crawled to a deserted nook
with a clan of memories asleep under
a heap of regrets
If you find a smile among your thoughts
tell it:
Our lips don't want to open
But if only, in the stream of our teary whispers,
one day,
it might give our words some color

Qaws 1380 / Sagittarius 2001

باغ من

دوست دارم معنی امید را باور کنم
راه غم بربندم و فکر ره دیگر کنم

ریشه های زنده گی را آبیاری لازم است
بعد ازین آینده را نوشاب در ساغر کنم

چشمه مهتاب را در سایه ها جاری کنم
سرو ها و سبزه ها را سبز در اختر کنم

باغ من در روشنی رشک گهرها میشود
گر گل خورشید را دعوت به این محشر کنم

روزگار از کار من افسانه ها خواهد نوشت
دوست دارم سینه تاریخ را پر زر کنم

انجمن گر در سرودنها مرا یاری کند
شعر ناب خویش را آذین هر دفتر کنم

جدی ۱۳۷۹

My Garden

I will trust the meaning of hope
I will shut the door on grief and find another path

Life's roots need water
I will raise my glass to drink to the future

I will let moonlight's spring flow through shadows
I will grow cypress trees even in the stars

If I invite lilies to this affair
I will make gems envy my garden

In time my work will be legendary
I will fill the chest of history with gold

If Anjuman helps me write these verses
I will gild every book with pure poetry

Jaddi 1379 / Capricorn 2000

زندان

درین سرای سکوت
یکی نمانده که دل خو کند به آوازش
زباغ سوخته‌اش بوی دود میآید
و سروهای رسایش در انتظار زلزله اند
که سر به خاک نهند
دریغ از آن که به پایان رسیده آغازش

هرآنکه بال و پری دارد و توانایی
به سان تیر ازین بی‌نشان گریزان است
به وقت بال‌گشایی و لحظه‌های فرار

خوش است حالت شوق عجیب پروازش
و آنکه قوت پرواز خود نمیبیند
فتاده گوشه‌یی ویرانه در پریشانی
کجاست یار سخنساز و قصه پردازش
درین سرای سکوت
امیدها همه در انتظار میمیرند

Prison

There is no one left
in this house of silence to hear her song
The smell of smoke drifts from her burnt garden
where her grand cypresses wait for the earthquake
that will bring their heads to the earth
How tragic that her beginning has come to an end

Anyone who has feathers and the strength
flees in an instant—she spreads her wings
and shoots from this nameless place like an arrow

The rare thrill of her flight is satisfying
She who doesn't find the strength to fly
suffers, prone, in a corner of ruins
Where did he go, the friend who told her stories?
In this house of silence
hopes die from waiting

نهالها همه در نوبهار میمیرند
به هرکه مینگری
به خود شکسته ز تکرار روزها سیراست
طلوع نیز ازین بخت تیره دلگیر است

ازین سرای خموشان و بی‌سرانجامان
فرار باید کرد
به سوی شهر افقهای دور و ناپیدا
به هر کجا که هیاهوی زیستن باشد
اگر که بال نباشد
به پای باید رفت
و پا اگر نبود دست دل به دریا زد
به آب باید زد
زباد باید خواست
ز هر رهی که میسر بود ازین زندان
فرار باید کرد
فرار باید کرد

دلو ۱۳۷۹

saplings die even in spring
In every face you see
is a person, broken, fed up with the tedium of days
Even the sunrise is solemn with its dark fate

You have to escape
from this cursed house of silence
to a city of far and invisible horizons
where there is the clamor of life
If you have no wings
go on foot
If you have no legs, leap into the dark
You must plunge into the sea
You must ask the wind
By any path that can lead away from this prison
you have to escape
you have to escape

Dalvæ 1379 / Aquarius 2001

Contributors

Aria Aber was born and raised in Germany and now lives in the United States. Her debut poetry collection, *Hard Damage*, won the Prairie Schooner Book Prize and the Whiting Award. She is a former Wallace Stegner Fellow at Stanford and graduate student at USC, and her writing has appeared in *The New Yorker*, *New Republic*, *The Yale Review*, *Granta*, and elsewhere. Raised speaking Persian and German, she writes in her third language, English. She recently joined the faculty of the University of Vermont as an assistant professor of Creative Writing and divides her time between Vermont and Brooklyn. Her debut novel, *Good Girl*, came out earlier this year.

Born in Herat, Afghanistan, **Nadia Anjuman** (1980–2005) surreptitiously gathered with women to discuss literature under the guise of practicing needlepoint. After Afghanistan's liberation from the Taliban, Anjuman attended Herat University and published *Gul-e-Dodi* (*Flower of Smoke*). She died in 2005 after being severely beaten by her husband. Her second volume of poetry, *Yek Sàbad Délhoreh* (*A Basket of Doubt*), was published the following year. *Flower of Smoke* has sold over three thousand copies.

Diana Arterian holds a PhD in literature & creative writing from the University of Southern California and is the author of the poetry collections *Agrippina the Younger* (Northwestern University Press) and *Playing Monster :: Seiche*, which received a starred review in *Publishers Weekly*. A poetry editor at Noemi Press, she writes "The Annotated Nightstand" column at *LitHub* and lives in Los Angeles.

Born in Argentina and raised bilingually in California, **Samantha Cosentino** explores the interior and exterior landscapes of migration, home, and identity in her creative work. Cosentino holds an MFA in creative writing and has taught in colleges, universities, and schools in the US and abroad. She has published poetry and translation in *Asymptote*, *New American Writing*, and elsewhere. Cosentino lives in the San Francisco Bay Area, where she writes, translates, and works in education.

Armen Davoudian is the author of *The Palace of Forty Pillars* (Tin House, 2024), longlisted for the National Book Critics Circle

Award in Poetry, and the translator, from Persian, of *Hopscotch* by Fatemeh Shams (Ugly Duckling Presse, 2024).

Hajar Hussaini is the author of *Disbound: Poems* (University of Iowa Press, 2022). She translated *Death and His Brother: A Novel* by Khosraw Mani (Syracuse University Press, 2026) from Persian, and her proposal to translate Maral Taheri's poetry collection won the Mo Habib Translation Prize in Persian Literature and will be published by Deep Vellum in 2026. A graduate of the Iowa Writers' Workshop, she is the visiting assistant professor of English at Skidmore College.

Mahbouba Ibrahimi was born in Kandahar, Afghanistan, in 1977. She immigrated to Sweden in 2011, where she currently works in the city of Uppsala as a Persian-language instructor and translator. Ibrahimi has published three poetry collections: بادها خواهران من‌اند [Winds are my sisters] (Tehran, 1990), مجنون، لیلی و بچه‌ها [Majnun, Layli, and the children] (Kabul, 2017), and به دهانم در آینه نگاه می‌کنی [You look at my mouth in the mirror] (Kabul, 2021).

Born in Baghlan, Afghanistan, human rights activist **Mariam Meetra** studied journalism in Kabul and earned an MS in sociology in Berlin. Her first book of poems was published in

Farsi. Meetra's poetry collection *Ich habe den Zorn des Windes gesehen* was published in a bilingual German-Dari edition and received the Adelbert von Chamisso Literary Prize. Meetra is a leading voice of Afghan poetry in exile. She works at Leipzig University and as a literary curator.

Sabrina Nouri grew up in Kabul and Paris. She holds an MA in language arts and a BA in Iranian studies from the Sorbonne University. Nouri has introduced several new Afghan authors and translated their novels into French. She has been awarded the Amédée-Pichot Prize and the Inalco Prize. Her translation *La Frontière des Oubliés* became the first work by an Iranian-Afghan author to be published by Gallimard. She currently lives in San Francisco.

Zuzanna Olszewska is an associate professor of social anthropology of the Middle East at the University of Oxford and a fellow of St. John's College. She is the author of the award-winning ethnography *The Pearl of Dari: Poetry and Personhood among Young Afghans in Iran* (Indiana University Press, 2015), as well as numerous articles and translations of Persian-language Afghan poetry.

Marina Omar moved to the US from Afghanistan in 2001 and received her PhD in political science from the University of Virginia in 2016. Marina has published an article on Afghan constitution selection in *British Journal of Middle Eastern Studies.* Her research has been supported by multiple fellowships and grants, including The Buckner W. Clay Endowment for the Humanities Fellowship, The Robert J. Huskey Travel Fellowship, and Quandt International Research Fund.

Born in Baharak, Afghanistan, **Karima Shabrang** holds a BA in Persian language and literature from Kabul University and published her first poetry collection at age twenty-four to much acclaim. She writes poetry that asserts her right to express her femininity. She has published five poetry collections in Persian, for which she has received numerous awards. Shabrang now lives in Berlin. A selection of her poems has been translated into German and published in an anthology.

Fatemeh Shams is the author of *When They Broke Down the Door* (Mage Publishers, 2016), translated by Dick Davis, and *Hopscotch* (Ugly Duckling Presse, 2024), translated by Armen Davoudian. She teaches Persian literature at the University of Pennsylvania.

Maral Taheri is a poet from Afghanistan. Her poetry collection translated from Persian to English by Hajar Hussaini won the 2024 Mo Habib Translation Prize in Persian Literature and will be published by Deep Vellum in 2026. As an activist, she was involved in women's rights movements in Iran and Afghanistan, working with independent and nonprofit campaigns. In the aftermath of the fall of Kabul and the start of the Woman, Life, Freedom movement in Iran, she left Iran and is now based in France.

Other titles in the Calico Series

That We May Live: Speculative Chinese Fiction

Home: Arabic Poems

Elemental: Earth Stories

Cuíer: Queer Brazil

This Is Us Losing Count: Eight Russian Poets

Visible: Text + Image

No Edges: Swahili Stories

Elektrik: Caribbean Writing

Through the Night Like a Snake: Latin American Horror Stories

Cigarettes Until Tomorrow: Romanian Poetry

Unusual Fragments : Japanese Stories

CALICO

The Calico Series, published biannually by Two Lines Press, captures vanguard works of translated literature in stylish, collectible editions. Each Calico is a vibrant snapshot that explores one aspect of our present moment, offering the voices of previously inaccessible, highly innovative writers from around the world today.